THiS JOURNAL BELONGS TO

____

____

www.ingramcontent.com/pod-product-compliance
Lightning Source LLC
Chambersburg PA
CBHW070545160726
48003CB00005B/1900